Saint John of the Cross

John of the Cross was born in 1542 in the small town of Fontiveros, near Ávila. He attended the Jesuit College in Medina del Campo, and then entered the Carmelite order in 1563, after which he spent four years studying Arts and Theology in the University of Salamanca. In 1567 he met Teresa of Ávila, and agreed to join her reform of the Carmelite order. Ten years later, in the winter of 1577, he was kidnapped by opponents of the Reform, and held in solitary confinement for nine months. During this time he wrote some of his finest poems. After escaping in the summer of 1578, he went to Andalusia, where he continued the work of the Reform and wrote commentaries on his three major poems, *En una noche oscura* (On a dark night), *Cántico espiritual* (Spiritual Canticle) and *¡Oh llama de amor viva!* (O living flame of love!). In 1588 he was appointed prior of the Carmelite house in Segovia, a position he held for three years, after which he returned to Andalusia, where he died in Úbeda in 1591. He was canonized in 1726, and in 1926 he was declared a Doctor of the Church.

Terence O'Reilly (1947–2023) was Professor Emeritus of Spanish at University College Cork and a member of the Royal Irish Academy.

Saint John of the Cross

Wisdom Sayings

Translated by

Terence O'Reilly

Iona is an imprint of Prosperity Education Limited
Registered offices: 58 Sherlock Close, Cambridge CB3 0HP, United Kingdom

First published 2021; revised 2023

A catalogue record for this book is available from the British Library

ISBN: 978-1-913825-93-5

Frontispiece: Drawing of the Crucifixion by St. John of the Cross, c.1550, via Wikimedia Commons

Typeset in Palatino 10pt by ORP Cambridge

For further information visit: www.prosperityeducation.net

Ad infinitum et ultra.

For Rachel and Ken

Contents

Preface

To the men and women he was guiding along a spiritual path John of the Cross occasionally gave *apophthegmata* (wisdom sayings) for them to ponder prayerfully and make their own. The practice had a long history in the monastic tradition, inspired by the sayings of the desert fathers. At some point he gathered together about eighty of his apophthegms, and wrote them out in a manuscript (*el manuscrito de Andújar*) that survives to this day. He also penned a short prologue to explain his purpose. Many people, he observed, wished to follow in the footsteps of Christ and thought they were doing so, when in fact they were stumbling on the path and going astray. They lacked discretion, a proper understanding of what it means to become like Jesus 'in one's life, conditions and virtues and in the form of nakedness and purity of one's spirit'. He prayed that his sayings might help them: 'You, Lord, love discretion, you love light, you love love more than the other operations of the soul; these sayings, therefore, will provide discretion for the journey, light for the road journeyed, and love in the journeying'.

In addition to the sayings in the Andújar manuscript, we possess others collected by the Carmelite nuns and friars who knew St John, bringing the total number that have survived to just under two hundred. They demand to be read, like Scripture, in a contemplative way: devoutly, thoughtfully and repeatedly, with a view to discerning God's will. Many were composed for women, notably the Carmelite sisters in Beas, near Granada, whom he knew well. These and others take for granted a communal life in which continuous prayer is prized, along with solitude, silence and seclusion, the conditions that enable it. But though they were written for enclosed religious, the practical wisdom they convey may be lived, with due allowance, outside the cloister too, for it is an expression of love. In his prologue St John describes them as, 'sayings of light and love' (*dichos de luz y amor*). He disclaims any pretension to human wisdom or eloquence: 'let worldly rhetoric', he writes, 'stand far off'; instead, 'let us speak to the heart words bathed in sweetness and love'. Implicit in the sayings, and voiced powerfully in some, is love of Christ, in whom, St John affirms, he has received 'everything I desire' (Saying 26).

Translating the sayings of St John is no easy task because of the skill with which he fashioned them. They are designed to catch the reader's attention, and to provoke thought. They take various forms, including plain statement, exclamation, admonition and prayer, and they are usually arresting, sometimes disturbing, and often puzzling or moving too. I have tried to reproduce in my versions the features of imagery, cadence and tone by which their effects are achieved, and in order to encourage a meditative reading of the kind St John desired, I have adapted the way Scripture was presented in the bibles of his time (*per cola et commata*) and have divided the text throughout into the semantic units that compose it.

My thanks are due to Nicholas Madden O.C.D. and Anne Walshe, who read earlier versions of the text, and to Tom O'Reilly for his advice and assistance at every stage.

Terence O'Reilly

The Wisdom Sayings of Saint John of the Cross

Prologue*

También, ¡oh Dios y deleite mío!, en estos dichos de luz y amor de ti se quiso mi alma emplear por amor de ti, porque ya que yo, teniendo la lengua de ellos, no tengo la obra y virtud de ellos, que es con lo que, Señor mío, te agradas, más que con el lenguaje y sabiduría de ellos, otras personas, provocadas por ellos, por ventura aprovechen en tu servicio y amor, en que yo falto, y tenga mi alma en qué se consolar de que haya sido ocasión que lo que falta en ella halles en otros.

Amas tú, Señor, la discreción, amas la luz, amas el amor sobre las demás operaciones del alma; por eso, estos dichos serán de discreción para el caminar, de luz para el camino y de amor en el caminar.

Quédese, pues, lejos la retórica del mundo; quédense las parlerías y elocuencia seca de la humana sabiduría, flaca e ingeniosa, de que nunca tú gustas, y hablemos palabras al corazón bañadas en dulzor y amor, de que tú bien gustas, quitando por ventura delante ofendículos y tropiezos a muchas almas que tropiezan no sabiendo, y no sabiendo van errando, pensando que aciertan en lo que es seguir a tu dulcísimo Hijo, Nuestro Señor Jesucristo, y hacerse semejantes a él en la vida, condiciones y virtudes y en la forma de la desnudez y pureza de su espirítu; mas dala tú, Padre de misericordias, porque sin ti no se hará nada, Señor.

O God my delight, for love of you
my soul has chosen to be busied also
with these sayings of light and love of you,

* St John did not include this prologue in the Andújar manuscript. It is taken from early manuscript copies of the sayings that Andújar includes. Nor did he provide a title in Andújar, though his reference in the prologue to *dichos de luz y amor* (sayings of light and love) is often applied in modern editions not only to the sayings in Andújar but to all those that have survived.

for though, possessing words for them,
I lack their deeds and virtue
(which please you more, my Lord,
than their expression and wisdom),
it may be that others, prompted by them,
will make progress in your service and love,
in which I am wanting,
and my soul be consoled that it has served as the means
of you finding in others what it lacks in itself.

You, Lord, love discretion, you love light,
you love love more than the other operations of the soul;
these sayings, therefore, will provide discretion for the journey,
light for the road journeyed, and love in the journeying.

Let worldly rhetoric, then, stand far off;
far off the chatter and dry eloquence
of human wisdom, feeble and contrived,
which never pleases you,
and let us speak to the heart
words bathed in sweetness and love,
which please you greatly,
in that way removing, perhaps,
obstacles and causes of stumbling
in the path of many souls
who stumble because they are ignorant
and in ignorance go astray,
thinking they are carrying out correctly what is involved
in following your most dear Son, our Lord Jesus Christ,
and becoming like him in one's life, conditions and virtues
and in the form of nakedness and purity of one's spirit;
but it is for you to grant this, Father of mercies,
for without you, Lord, nothing will be achieved.

The Autograph Manuscript of Andújar*

* The manuscript takes its name from Andújar (Jaén), where it is conserved in the church of Santa María la Mayor. There is a paleographic transcription of the text in Lucinio (1984: 159–63), and a facsimile edition, *San Juan de la Cruz, Dichos de Luz y Amor, edición facsímil (Códice de Andújar)*, edited by José Vicente Rodríguez (Madrid: Editorial de Espiritualidad, 1976).

1. *Siempre el Señor descubrió los tesoros de su sabiduría y espíritu a los mortales, mas ahora que la malicia va descubriendo más su cara, mucho los descubre.*[1]

The Lord has always disclosed to mortals
the secrets of his wisdom and spirit,
but now that Evil is uncovering more of its face,
he is disclosing them abundantly.

2. *O Señor, Dios mío, ¿quién te buscará con amor puro y sencillo que te deje de hallar muy a su gusto y voluntad, pues que tú te muestras primero y sales al encuentro a los que te desean?*[2]

O Lord, my God,
will anyone who seeks you
with love that is pure and simple
fail to find you
just as they please and wish?
For you are the first to show yourself,
and you go out to meet those who desire you.

3. *Aunque el camino es llano y suave para los hombres de buena voluntad, el que camina caminará poco y con trabajo si no tiene buenos pies y ánimo y porfía animosa en eso mismo.*

Though the road is level and smooth
for those who have goodwill,
the person travelling will advance little

1 Some manuscripts read 'mucho más' (more abundantly).

2 An allusion, perhaps, to the parable of the Prodigal Son, where the father runs to meet his son while he is 'yet a great way off' (Luke 15.20). See too Wisdom 1.1–2: 'seek him in simplicity of heart. For he is found by them that tempt him not: and he sheweth himself to them that have faith in him'.

and with difficulty
if they lack strong legs and courage
and courageous perseverance on the way.

4. *Más vale estar cargado junto al fuerte que aliviado junto al flaco; cuando estás cargado, estás junto a Dios que es tu fortaleza, el cual está con los atribulados;*[3] *cuando estás aliviado, estás junto a ti que eres tu misma flaqueza; porque la virtud y fuerza del alma en los trabajos de paciencia crece y se confirma.*

It is better to be burdened next to someone strong
than without a burden next to someone weak:
when you are burdened you are next to God
who is your strength,
and who accompanies those who are suffering;
when you have no burden you are next to yourself,
and you are your weakness:
for in troubles that require patience
the virtue and strength of the soul
are increased and confirmed.

5. *El que solo se quiere estar, sin arrimo de maestro y guía, será como el árbol que está solo y sin dueño en el campo, que, por más fruto que tenga, los viadores se la cogerán y no llegará a sazón.*

The person who wishes to be alone,
without the support of a master and guide,
will end up like the tree in open country
that has no owner:

3 2 Corinthians 12.9: 'And he said to me: My grace is sufficient for thee; for power is made perfect in infirmity. Gladly therefore will I glory in my infirmities, that the power of Christ may dwell in me'.

however fruitful it may be,
passers-by will strip it,
and it will not reach maturity.

6. *El árbol cultivado y guardado con el beneficio de su dueño da la fruta en el tiempo que de él se espera.*

The tree that is cultivated and protected
is enabled by the care of its owner
to bear fruit at the expected time.

7. *El alma sola, sin maestro, que tiene virtud, es como el carbón encendido que está solo: antes se irá enfriando que encendiendo.*

The soul that is alone,
without a master, and living virtuously,
is like a burning coal that is alone:
it is more likely to grow colder than hotter.

8. *El que a solas cae, a solas se está caído, y tiene en poco su alma, pues de sí solo la fía.*

The person who falls when alone
lies alone on the ground,
and attaches little value to their soul,
since they entrust it to themselves alone.

9. *Pues no temes el caer a solas, ¿cómo presumes de levantarte a solas? Mira que más pueden dos juntos que uno solo.*[4]

Seeing you are not afraid of falling when alone,

---

4 Ecclesiastes 4.9–10: 'It is better therefore that two should be together, than one: for they have the advantage of their society: if one fall he shall be supported by the other: woe to him that is alone, for when he falleth, he hath none to lift him up'.

how do you expect to get up when alone?
Note that two people can do more together
than one person by himself.

10. *El que cargado cae, dificultosamente se levantará cargado.*

The person who falls when burdened,
will find it hard to get up burdened.

11. *Y el que cae ciego, no se levantará ciego solo; y si se levantare solo, encaminará por donde no conviene.*

And the person who falls in their blindness,
will not get up alone in their blindness;
and if they do get up alone,
they will wander into unsuitable places.

12. *Más quiere Dios de ti el menor grado de pureza de conciencia que cuantas obras puedes hacer.*

God would rather find in you
the lowest degree of purity of conscience
than all the good works you can do.

13. *Más quiere Dios en ti el menor grado de obediencia y sujeción que todos esos servicios que le piensas hacer.*[5]

God would rather find in you
the lowest degree of obedience and submission
than all those services
you are planning to render him.

5 1 Samuel 15.22: 'And Samuel said: Doth the Lord desire holocausts and victims, and not rather that the voice of the Lord should be obeyed? For obedience is better than sacrifices: and to hearken rather than to offer the fat of rams'.

14. *Más estima Dios en ti el inclinarte a la sequedad y el padecer por su amor que todas las consolaciones y visiones espirituales y meditaciones que puedas tener.*

God would rather find in you an inclination
to experience dryness and suffering for love of him
than all the consolations, spiritual visions and meditations
you could possibly have.

15. *Niega tus deseos y hallarás lo que desea tu corazón; ¿qué sabes tú si tu apetito es según Dios?*

Renounce your desires
and you will find your heart's desire;
how can you be sure
that your appetite accords with God?

16. *¡O dulcísimo amor de Dios mal conocido! El que halló sus venas descansó.*

O most joyous love of God,
so poorly understood!
The person who has found
the veins of this mine
has entered into rest.

17. *Pues se te ha de seguir doblada armagura de cumplir tu voluntad, no la quieras seguir, aunque quedes en armagura.*

Since doing your own will is sure to bring you
a double dose of bitterness,
choose not to follow it, even if
you end up feeling bitter.

18. *Más indecencia e impureza lleva el alma para ir a Dios si lleva en sí el menor apetito de cosa del mundo que si fuese cargada de todas las feas y molestas tentaciones y tinieblas que se pueden decir, con tal que su voluntad razonal no las quiera admitir; antes el tal entonces puede confiadamente llegar a Dios por hacer la voluntad de su Majestad que dice, 'Venid a mí todos los que estáis trabajados y cargados y yo os recrearé'.*[6]

If the soul is carrying within itself
the slightest appetite for something in the world,
it is carrying more filth and impurity
on its way to God
than if it were weighed down
by all the ugly and troublesome temptations and darkness
that can possibly be described
provided that its rational will refuses to admit them;
indeed, the person concerned
may then approach God confidently,
because they are doing the will of his Majesty who says:
'Come to me all you who are suffering and burdened
and I shall refresh you'.

19. *Más agrada a Dios el alma que con sequedad y trabajo se sujeta a lo que es razón que la que, faltando en esto, hace todas sus cosas con consolación.*

The soul that in dryness and with difficulty
subjects itself to what accords with reason
is more pleasing to God
than one who, failing to do this,
acts in all things with consolation.

6 Matthew 11.28.

20. *Más agrada a Dios una obra, por pequeña que sea, hecha en escondido, no teniendo voluntad de que se sepa, que mil hechas con gana de que las sepan los hombres. Porque el que con purísimo amor obra por Dios, no solamente no se le da nada de que lo vean los hombres, pero ni lo hace porque lo sepa el mismo Dios; el cual, aunque nunca lo hubiese de saber, no cesaría de hacerle los mismos servicios con la misma alegría y pureza de amor.*[7]

God is more pleased with one good act, however small,
carried out in seclusion,
without any desire for it to be known,
than a thousand performed with a wish
for others to know them.
For someone who with a most pure love
performs a good act for God,
not only cares nothing about others seeing it,
but does not do it for God himself to know;
even if He were never to know it, such a person
would not cease to serve Him in the same ways,
with the same happiness and pure love.

21. *La obra pura y entera, hecha por Dios, en el seno puro hace reino entero para su dueño.*

A good action that is pure and complete,
and performed for God,
provides in the breast that is pure
a complete kingdom for its master.

22. *Dos veces trabaja el pájaro que se asentó en la liga, es a saber, en desasirse y limpiarse de ella; y de dos maneras*

7 See Matthew 6.1–6.

pena el que cumple su apetito: en desasirse, y, después de desasido, en purgarse de lo que de él se le pegó.

The bird that has landed in birdlime has two tasks,
namely to become free of it
and then to clean itself;
and the person who satisfies their appetite suffers twice:
to struggle free and, once free,
to shed what has stuck to them.

23. *El que de los apetitos no se deja llevar volará ligero según el espíritu, como el ave a que no falta pluma.*

The person who does not allow
their appetites to carry them away
will fly light in spirit, like a bird
that has no lack of feathers.

24. *La mosca que a la miel se arrima impide su vuelo; y el alma que se quiere estar asida al sabor del espíritu impide su libertad y contemplación.*

The fly that clings to honey
impedes its own flight;
and the soul whose wish it is
to cling to sweetness of spirit
impedes its freedom and contemplation.

25. *No te hagas presente a las criaturas si quieres guardar el rostro de Dios claro y sencillo en tu alma, mas vacía y enajena mucho tu espíritu de ellas y andarás en divinas luces, porque Dios no es semejante a ellas.*

Do not make yourself present to created things
if you wish to keep God's face
clear and simple in your soul;
instead make your spirit empty of them
and far distant from them
and you will walk in light that is divine,
for God is not like them.

26. *Oración de Alma Enamorada* | Prayer of a Soul in Love

¡Señor Dios, amado mío! Si todavía te acuerdas de mis pecados para no hacer lo que te ando pidiendo, haz en ellos, Dios mío, tu voluntad, que es lo que yo más quiero, y ejercita tu bondad y misericordia y serás conocido en ellos.

Lord God, my beloved:
if the memory of my sins still prevents you
from doing what I am asking,
may your will, my God, be done in them,
which is what I most desire,
and exercise your goodness and mercy,
and in them you will be made known.

Y si es que esperas a mis obras para por ese medio concederme mi ruego, dámelas tú y óbramelas, y las penas que tú quisieres aceptar, y hágase.

And if you are waiting for my deeds
so as to grant me in that way my request,
give them to me yourself
and accomplish them for me
with whatever trials you wish to accept,
and do so now.

Y si a las obras mías no esperas, ¿qué esperas, clementísimo Señor mío? ¿Por qué te tardas?

And if you are not waiting for my deeds,
what are you waiting for my most merciful Lord?
Why do you delay?

Porque si, en fin, ha de ser gracia y misericordia la que en tu Hijo te pido, toma mi cornadillo, pues le quieres, y dame este bien, pues que tú también lo quieres.

For if what I am requesting in your Son
has, in the end, to be grace and mercy,
take my poor offering, since you desire it,
and grant me this good, since you desire it as well.

¿Quién se podrá librar de los modos y términos bajos, si no le levantas tú a ti en pureza de amor, Dios mío? ¿Cómo se levantará a ti el hombre, engendrado y criado en bajezas, si no le levantas tú, Señor, con la mano que le hiciste?[8]

Who can become free
of lowly means and ends
unless lifted up by you to yourself
in love that is pure, my God?
How can humans, conceived and reared in corruption,
rise up to you,
unless, Lord, you raise them up yourself,
with the hand you have fashioned for them?

8 The 'hand' may be an allusion to Christ: cf. Cassiodorus, *Patrologia Latina*, vol. 70, col. 976: 'The right hand of those who are good is Christ our Lord, as it says in Psalm 15.8, "I set the Lord always in my sight: for he is at my right hand, that I be not moved" (*Dextra quippe bonorum est Christus Dominus, sicut in quintodecimo psalmo dictum est: 'Providebam Dominum in conspectu meo semper, quoniam a dextris est mihi, ne commovear*').

No me quitarás, Dios mío, lo que una vez me diste en tu único Hijo Jesucristo, en que me diste todo lo que quiero; por eso me holgaré, que no te tardarás si yo espero.

You will not take from me, my God,
what you once gave me
in your only Son Jesus Christ,
in whom you gave me everything I desire;
therefore I will rejoice,
for you will not delay, if I am waiting.

¿Con qué dilaciones esperas, pues desde luego puedes amar a Dios en tu corazón?[9]

Why these delays while you are waiting,
when you can love God right now in your heart?

Míos son los cielos y mía es la tierra; mías son las gentes, los justos son míos y míos los pecadores; los ángeles son míos, y la Madre de Dios, y todas las cosas son mías, y el mismo Dios es mío y para mí, porque Cristo es mío y todo para mí. Pues, ¿qué pides y buscas, alma mía? Tuyo es todo esto, y todo es para ti.[10] *No te pongas en menos ni repares en meajas que se caen de la mesa de tu Padre.*[11]

Mine are the heavens and mine is the earth;
mine are all peoples,
the just are mine and mine are the sinful;
the angels are mine,

9 Pacho (1997: 96) ends at this point the *Cancion de alma enamorada*, and makes the remaining two points into a separate saying, which he numbers 27. I have followed the divisions and numbering in Lucinio (1994: 156) and Rodríguez (1993: 98).

10 1 Corinthians 3.22–23: 'For all things are yours, whether it be Paul, or Apollo, or Cephas, or the world, or life, or death, or things present, or things to come; for all are yours; and you are Christ's; and Christ is God's'.

11 An allusion to the words addressed by the Canaanite woman to Christ in Matthew 15.26–27.

and the Mother of God,
and all things are mine,
and God himself is mine, and for me,
because Christ is mine, and for me entirely.
What then, my soul, are you asking for and seeking?
All this is yours, and all things are for you.
Do not underrate your worth
or pay attention to crumbs
falling from your Father's table.

Sal fuera y gloríate en tu gloria; escóndete en ella y goza, y alcanzarás las peticiones de tu corazón.[12]

Go forth and glory in the glory that is yours;
hide within it and rejoice,
and you will obtain what you ask for in your heart.

27. *El espíritu bien puro no se mezcla con extrañas advertencias ni humanos respetos, sino solo, en soledad de todas las formas, interiormente, con sosiego sabroso, se comunica con Dios, porque su conocimiento es en silencio divino.*

A spirit that is truly pure
has nothing to do with random distractions
or human respect,
but in solitude, removed from all outward appearances,
inwardly, and with delightful tranquility,
it communicates with God,
for it is in divine silence that he is known.

12 Psalm 36.4: 'Delight in the Lord, and he will give thee the requests of thy heart'.

28. *El alma enamorada es alma blanda, mansa, humilde y paciente.*

A soul in love is a gentle soul,
meek, humble and patient.

29. *El alma dura en su amor propio se endurece.*

A soul that is hard
in self-love is hardened.

30. *Si tú en tu amor, ¡oh buen Jesús!, no suavizas el alma, siempre perseverará en su natural dureza.*

If you in your love, oh good Jesus,
do not soften the soul,
it will continue for ever
in its natural hardness.

31. *El que la ocasión pierde es como el que soltó el ave de la mano, que no la volverá*[13] *a cobrar.*

The person who wastes an opportunity
is like someone
who has let go of a bird in their hand:
they won't get it back again.

32. *No te conocía yo a ti,oh Señor mío, porque todavía quería saber y gustar cosas.*

I did not know you, my Lord,
because I still wished
to know things and to taste them.

13 Lucinio (1994: 161) reads 'boluerás'.

33. *Múdese todo muy enhorabuena, Señor Dios, porque hagamos asiento en ti.*

Change in everything is welcome, Lord God,
if it makes us find our rest in you.

34. *Un solo pensamiento del hombre vale más que todo el mundo; por tanto, sólo Dios es digno de él.*

One thought of a human being
is worth more than the whole world;
for that reason
only God is worthy of it.

35. *Para lo insensible, lo que no sientes; para lo sensible, el sentido, y para el espíritu de Dios, el pensamiento.*

Direct to what does not have feeling
what you do not feel,
to what does have feeling, your sensibility,
and to God's spirit, your thoughts.

36. *Mira que tu ángel custodio no siempre mueve el apetito a obrar, aunque siempre alumbra la razón; por tanto, para obrar virtud no esperes al gusto, que bástate la razón y entendimiento.*

Note that your guardian angel
does not always prompt your appetite into action,
though it always enlightens your reason;
therefore to perform a good act
do not wait on feeling,
since reason and understanding are enough.

37. *No da lugar el apetito a que le mueva el ángel cuando está puesto en otra cosa.*

Your appetite does not let the angel prompt it
while it is turned towards something elsewhere.

38. *Secado se ha mi espíritu, porque se olvida*[14] *de apacentarse en ti.*

My spirit has become dry,
because it forgets
to draw nourishment from you.

39. *Eso que pretendes y lo que más deseas no lo hallarás por esa vía tuya ni por la alta contemplación, sino en la mucha humildad y rendimiento de corazón.*

What you are seeking and what you most desire
you will not find by following that way of yours
nor by profound contemplation,
but in great humility and surrender of heart.

40. *No te canses, que no entrarás en el sabor y suavidad de espíritu si no te dieres a la mortificación de todo eso que quieres.*

Do not tire yourself, for you will not enter
delight and evenness of spirit
unless you begin to renounce
all those things you desire.

41. *Mira que la flor más delicada más presto se marchita y pierde su olor; por tanto, guárdate de querer caminar por*

14 Rodríguez (1993: 99) reads 'olvidó'.

espíritu de sabor, porque no serás constante; mas escoge para ti un espíritu robusto, no asido a nada, y hallarás dulzura y paz en abundancia; porque la sabrosa y durable fruta en tierra fría y seca se coge.

Note that the most delicate flower
becomes withered and unscented most quickly;
make sure therefore that you do not choose
to journey in spiritual delight,
because you will not persevere;
but make your own a spirit that is robust,
attached to nothing,
and you will find an abundance of sweetness and peace;
for tasty and lasting fruit is picked
in ground that is cold and dry.

42. *Cata que tu carne es flaca*[15] *y que ninguna cosa del mundo puede dar fortaleza a tu espíritu ni consuelo, porque lo que nace del mundo, mundo es, y lo que nace de la carne, carne es: y el buen espíritu sólo nace del espíritu de Dios,*[16] *que se comunica no por mundo ni carne.*

Be aware that your flesh is weak
and that nothing in the world can give
strength or solace to your spirit,
for what is born of the world is worldly,
and what is born of the flesh is flesh;
and a good spirit is born only from God's spirit,
which is not communicated by the world or the flesh.

15 Mark 14.38: 'The spirit indeed is willing, but the flesh is weak'.

16 John 3.6: 'That which is born of the flesh is flesh, and that which is born of the Spirit is spirit'.

43. *Entra en cuenta con tu razón para hacer lo que ella te dice en el camino de Dios, y valdráte más para con tu Dios que todas las obras que sin esta advertencia haces y que todos los sabores espirituales que pretendes.*

Come to terms with your reason
in order to do what it tells you
on the path to God,
and it will stand to you more
in the presence of your God
than all the works you perform
without bearing this in mind,
and more than all the spiritual delights
that you desire.

44. *Bienaventurado el que, dejado aparte su gusto e inclinación, mira las cosas en razón y justicia para hacerlas.*

Blessed is the person who leaving aside
their own pleasure and inclination
considers things with reason and justice
in order to carry them out.

45. *El que obra razón es como el que come sustancia, y el que se mueve por el gusto de su voluntad como el que come fruta floja.*

A person who acts according to reason
is like someone eating good food,
while someone who is moved
by the pleasure of their will
is like a person eating fruit that is tasteless.

46. *Tú, Señor, vuelves con alegría y amor a levantar al que te ofende, y yo no vuelvo a levantar y honrar al que me enoja a mí.*

You, Lord, turn back,
happily and lovingly,
to raise up the person who offends you,
while I do not turn back
to raise up and honour
the person with whom I am angry.

47. *¡O poderoso Señor!, si una centella del tu imperio de tu justicia*[17] *tanto hace en el príncipe mortal que gobierna y mueve las gentes, ¿qué hará tu omnipotente justicia sobre el justo y el pecador?*

O powerful Lord!
If one spark falling from the empire of your justice
has such an impact on a mortal prince
who governs peoples and directs them,
what will your all-powerful justice do
to a just person and one who is sinful?

48. *Si purificares tu alma de extrañas posesiones y apetitos, entenderás en espíritu las cosas, y si negares el apetito en ellas, gozarás de la verdad de ellas, entendiendo en ellas lo cierto.*

If you cleanse your soul
of alien possessions and appetites,
you will gain in your spirit
understanding of things,

17 Rodríguez (1993: 100) and Pacho (1997: 98) read, 'del imperio de tu justicia'. Lucinio's reading (1994: 157), which I reproduce, is the one in the manuscript.

and if in such things you renounce your appetite,
you will savour their truth,
understanding what in them is sure.

49. *Señor, Dios mío, no eres tú extraño a quien no se extraña contigo; ¿cómo dicen que te ausentas tú?*

Lord my God, you are no stranger
to one not estranged from you:
how then can they say
that you make yourself absent?

50. *Verdaderamente aquél tiene vencidas todas las cosas que ni el gusto de ellas le mueve a gozo ni el desabrimiento le causa tristeza.*

That person has truly mastered all things
who is not moved to joy
by the pleasure they afford
nor made dejected
when they are unpleasant.

51. *Si quieres venir al santo recogimiento, no has de venir admitiendo sino negando.*

If you wish to attain holy recollection,
the way there is not indulgence,
but renunciation.

52. *Yéndome yo, Dios mío, por doquiera contigo, por doquiera me irá como yo quiero para ti.*

If I go everywhere with you, my God,
then I will go everywhere
in the way I want for you.

53. *No podrá llegar a la perfección el que no procura satisfacerse con nonada, de manera que la concupiscencia natural y espiritual estén contentas en vacío; que para llegar a la suma tranquilidad y paz de espíritu esto se requiere; y, de esta manera, el amor de Dios en el alma pura y sencilla casi frecuentemente está en acto.*

A person cannot reach perfection
without trying to be satisfied with nothing,
so that their concupiscence, both natural and spiritual,
finds contentment in emptiness;
for to reach the highest degree
of spiritual tranquillity and peace
this is required;
and this way the love of God
in a soul that is pure and simple
is almost always active.

54. *Mira que, pues Dios es inaccesible, no repares en cuanto tus potencias pueden comprehender y tu sentido sentir, porque no te satisfagas con menos y pierda tu alma la ligereza conveniente para ir a él.*

Take care, since God is inaccessible,
not to focus on what your mind can grasp
or your spiritual sense feel,
else you will be content with less,
and your soul will lose the lightness
that helps it go to Him.

55. *Como el que tira el carro la cuesta arriba, así camina para Dios el alma que no sacude el cuidado y apaga el apetito.*

Like someone pulling a cart uphill

is a soul on its way to God
that does not shake off its cares
and extinguish its appetite.

56. *No es de voluntad de Dios que el alma se turbe de nada ni que padezca trabajos; que si los padece en los adversos casos del mundo es por la flaqueza de su virtud, porque el alma del perfecto se goza en lo que se pena la imperfecta.*

God does not wish the soul
to be disturbed about anything,
nor to endure trials;
and if it does endure them
in the adverse events of the world
it is because its virtue is weak,
for a soul that is perfect delights
in what makes one imperfect distressed.

57. *El camino de la vida de muy poco bullicio y negociación es, y más requiere mortificación de la voluntad que mucho saber; el que tomare de las cosas y gustos lo menos, andará más por él.*

The path that leads to life
is not at all busy
or hard to negotiate,
and rather than great knowledge
it requires a mortified will;
the person who takes least from things and pleasures
will travel further along it.

58. *No pienses que el agradar a Dios está tanto en obrar mucho como en obrarlo con buena voluntad, sin propiedad y respectos.*

Do not think that pleasing God involves many deeds
rather than deeds performed with goodwill,
without attachment or concern for what others think.

59. *A la tarde te examinarán en el amor. Aprende a amar como Dios quiere ser amado, y deja tu condición.*

In the evening you will be examined in love.
Learn how to love
as God wishes to be loved,
and forget about how you are.

60. *Cata que no te entremetas en cosas ajenas, ni aun las pases por tu memoria, porque quizá no podrás tú cumplir con tu tarea.*

Be careful not to involve yourself
in the affairs of other people;
do not even think about them,
else it may be you will not manage
to complete the task that is yours.

61. *No pienses que, porque en aquél no relucen las virtudes que tú piensas, no será precioso delante de Dios por lo que tú no piensas.*

Because a certain person does not shine
with the virtues you expect,
do not think that he or she
is not precious in the sight of God
for reasons you do not know.

62. *No sabe el hombre gozarse bien ni dolerse bien, porque no entiende la distancia del bien y del mal.*[18]

18 Ecclesiastes 6.5: 'He hath not seen the sun, nor known the distance of good and evil'.

People do not know how
to rejoice or grieve properly,
because they do not grasp the distance
between good and evil.

63. *Mira que no te entristezcas de repente de los casos adversos del siglo, pues que no sabes el bien que traen consigo ordenado en los juicios de Dios para el gozo sempiterno de los escogidos.*

Be careful that adverse events in the world
do not suddenly cast you down,
for you do not know the good
that they bring with them,
arranged in the designs of God
for the joy without end of the elect.

64. *No te goces en las prosperidades temporales, pues no sabes de cierto que te aseguran la vida eterna.*

Do not rejoice when temporal things prosper,
since you cannot be sure
they will secure you eternal life.

65. *En la tribulación acude luego a Dios confiadamente y serás esforzado y alumbrado y enseñado.*

When you are in distress
approach God at once with confidence,
and you will be given
strength, light and instruction.

66. *En los gozos y gustos acude luego a Dios con temor y verdad, y no serás engañado ni envuelto en vanidad.*

In joy and pleasure
approach God at once
with fear and in truth,
and you will not be misled
nor wrapped in vanity.

67. *Toma a Dios por esposo y amigo con quien te andes de contino,*[19] *y no pecarás, y sabrás amar, y haránse las cosas necesarias prósperamente para ti.*

Take God as a spouse and friend
with whom to walk continually;
then you will not sin,
and you will know how to love,
and everything you need
will prosper for you.

68. *Sin trabajo sujetarás las gentes y te servirán las cosas si te olvidares de ellas y de ti mismo.*

Without effort on your part
you will win people over
and things will serve you
if you forget them all
and yourself as well.

69. *Date al descanso echando de ti cuidados y no se te dando nada de cuanto acaece, y servirás a Dios a su gusto y holgarás en él.*

Give yourself a rest
by casting off your worries
and letting nothing that happens

19 Pacho (1997:100) has 'continuo'.

disturb you at all,
and you will serve God
just as He wishes
and in Him you will be at ease.

70. *Mira que no reina Dios sino en el alma pacífica y desinteresada.*

Note that God does not reign
except in a soul
that is peaceful and detached.

71. *Aunque obres muchas cosas, si no aprendes a negar tu voluntad y sujetarte, perdiendo cuidado de ti y de tus cosas, no aprovecharás en la perfección.*

You may be active in many ways,
but unless you learn to renounce your will
and to master yourself,
letting go of worry about yourself and your affairs,
you will not make progress in perfection.

72. *¿Qué aprovecha dar tú a Dios una cosa si él te pide otra? Considera lo que Dios querrá y hazlo, que por ahí satisfarás mejor tu corazón que con aquello a que tú te inclinas.*

What is the point of giving something to God
if He is asking you for something else?
Consider what God would like and do it,
and in that way you will make your heart more content
than by following your inclination.

73. *¿Cómo te atreves a holgarte tan sin temor, pues has de parecer delante de Dios a dar cuenta de la menor palabra y pensamiento?*

How do you dare
to enjoy yourself so fearlessly,
seeing you must stand before God
to give an account
for your least word and thought?

74. *Mira que son muchos los llamados y pocos los escogidos,*[20] *y que si tú de ti no tienes cuidado más cierta está tu perdición que tu remedio, mayormente siendo la senda que guía a la vida eterna tan estrecha.*[21]

Note that those called are many
and those chosen are few,
and that unless you take care
you are more likely to be lost than saved,
especially bearing in mind
that the path to life eternal is so narrow.

75. *No te alegres vanamente, pues sabes cuántos pecados has hecho y no sabes cómo está Dios contigo, sino teme con confianza.*

Do not rejoice without reason,
for you know how many are your sins,
but not how God views you;
instead be afraid with confidence.

76. *Pues que en la hora de la cuenta te ha de pesar de no haber empleado este tiempo en servicio de Dios, ¿por qué no le ordenas y empleas ahora como lo querrías haber hecho cuando te estés muriendo?*

---

20 Matthew 22.14

21 Matthew 7.14

Since at the hour of judgement
you will be distressed
that you did not use the present time
in God's service,
why not arrange and use it now
as you would wish to have done
when you are dying?

77. *Si quieres que en tu espíritu nazca la devoción y que crezca el amor de Dios y apetito de las cosas divinas, limpia el alma de todo apetito y asimiento y pretensión, de manera que no se te dé nada por nada; porque, así como el enfermo, echado fuera el mal humor, luego siente el bien de la salud y le nace gana de comer, así tú convalecerás en Dios si en lo dicho te curas; y sin ello, aunque más hagas, no aprovecharás.*

If you want devotion to be born in your soul,
with growth in your love of God
and in your appetite for heavenly things,
cleanse your soul
of every appetite, attachment and false ambition,
so that nothing at all causes you concern.
For just as someone sick, when the illness is over,
feels the return of health and an appetite for food,
so will you recover in God if you treat yourself thus;
otherwise, whatever you do, you will not make progress.

78. *Si deseas hallar la paz y consuelo de tu alma y servir a Dios de veras, no te contentes con eso que has dejado, porque por ventura te estás en lo que de nuevo andas tan impedido o más que antes; mas deja todas esas cosas que te quedan*[22] *y apártate a una sola*

22 Matthew 19.21: 'Jesus saith to him: If thou wilt be perfect, go sell what thou hast, and give to the poor, and thou shalt have treasure in heaven: and come follow me'.

que lo trae todo consigo,[23] *que es la soledad santa acompañada con oración y santa y divina lección, y allí persevera en olvido de todas las cosas; que, si de obligación no te incumben, más agradarás a Dios en saberte guardar y perfeccionar a ti mismo que en granjearlas todas juntas, porque ¿qué le aprovecha al hombre ganar todo el mundo si deja perder su alma?*[24]

If you desire to find
peace and solace for your soul
and to serve God truly,
do not be satisfied with those things
you have given up already,
for perhaps in your present state
you are just as hindered
as you were previously, or more;
but give up all you still possess,
and draw apart to the one thing
that brings everything with it,
namely a holy solitude,
accompanied by prayer
and by reading that is holy and divine,
and there persevere
in forgetfulness of all things,
for unless they concern you by duty,
you will please God more
by protecting and perfecting yourself
than by cultivating all things together;
since what does it profit a person
to gain the whole world
if it is at the cost of their soul?

23 Luke 10.42: 'one thing is necessary'.

24 Matthew 16.26.

Points of Love*

* The sayings in this section are found in early manuscripts and editions. Some of them (numbers 79–104) appear to have been written for the Carmelite sisters in Beas. Others (numbers 105 and 122–157) were published in a seventeenth-century collection, *Glosas a unos tercetos, sacados de los libros del V.P.F. Juan de la Cruz*, edited by Jerónimo de la Asunción (Gerona: Gerónimo Palol, 1650). See Rodríguez (1993: 91).

79. *Refrene mucho la lengua y el pensamiento y traiga de ordinario el afecto en Dios, y calentársele ha el espíritu divinamente.*

Keep a tight rein on your tongue and your thoughts,
and habitually place your affection in God,
and your spirit will be kindled divinely.

80. *No apaciente el espíritu en otra cosa que en Dios. Deseche las advertencias de las cosas, y traiga paz y recogimiento en el corazón.*

Do not feed your spirit except on God.
Expel distracting thoughts of things,
and draw peace and recollection into your heart.

81. *Traiga sosiego espiritual en advertencia de Dios amorosa, y cuando fuere necesario hablar, sea con el mismo sosiego y paz.*

Maintain a spiritual calm
by attending lovingly to God,
and when it is necessary to speak,
do so with the same calm and peace.

82. *Tenga ordinaria memoria de la vida eterna, y que los que más abatidos y pobres y en menos se tienen gozarán de más alto señorío y gloria en Dios.*[25]

Always keep in mind
the life that is eternal,
and that those who know themselves to be
most wretched, poor and lowly

25 Matthew 5.3: 'Blessed are the poor in spirit: for theirs is the kingdom of heaven'.

will enjoy in God
a higher place and glory.

83. *Alégrese ordinariamente en Dios, que es su salud,*[26] *y mire que es bueno el padecer de cualquiera manera por el que es bueno.*

Always rejoice in God,
who is your salvation,
and reflect that it is good
to suffer in any way
for the one who is good.

84. *Consideren cómo han menester ser enemigas de sí mismas y caminar por el santo rigor a la perfección, y entiendan que cada palabra que hablaren sin orden de obediencia se la pone Dios en cuenta.*[27]

Consider how you need
to be your own enemies
and to walk towards perfection
with a holy austerity,
and grasp that each word you utter
without being commanded by obedience
is taken account of by God.

85. *Intimo deseo de que Dios la dé lo que Su Majestad sabe que le falta para honra suya.*

Heartfelt desire that God will grant you
what His Majesty knows you need
to give him due honour.

26 Luke 1.47: 'my spirit hath rejoiced in God my Saviour'.

27 Matthew 12.36: 'every idle word that men shall speak, they shall render an account for it in the day of judgment'.

86. *Crucificada interior y exteriormente con Cristo, vivirá en esta vida con hartura y satisfacción de su alma, poseyéndola en su paciencia.*[28]

Crucified with Christ
inwardly and outwardly,
you will live in this life
with fullness and satisfaction in your soul,
possessing it in your patience.

87. *Traiga advertencia amorosa en Dios, sin apetito de querer sentir ni entender cosa particular de él.*

Attend lovingly to God,
without attachment to the desire
to feel or understand
something specific about him.

88. *Ordinaria confianza en Dios, estimando en sí y en las hermanas lo que Dios más estima, que son los bienes espirituales.*

Have confidence always in God,
valuing in yourself and the sisters
what God values most highly,
namely spiritual blessings.

89. *Entrese en su seno y trabaje en presencia del Esposo, que siempre está presente queriéndola bien.*

Enter into your heart
and work in the presence of your Spouse,
who is present always,
loving you dearly.

---

28 Luke 21.19: 'In your patience you shall possess your souls'.

90. *Sea enemiga de admitir en su alma cosas que no tienen en sí sustancia espiritual, porque no la hagan perder el gusto de la devoción y el recogimiento.*

Fight against admitting into your soul
things that in themselves lack spiritual substance,
to prevent them making you lose
the taste for devotion and recollection.

91. *Bástele Cristo crucificado, y con él pene y descanse, y por esto aniquilarse en todas las cosas exteriores e interiores.*

Be content with Christ crucified,
and with him suffer and rest,
and in that way be annihilated
in all things outward and interior.

92. *Procure siempre que las cosas no sean nada para ella, ni ella para las cosas; mas, olvidada de todo, more en su recogimiento con el Esposo.*

Ensure always that things mean nothing to you,
and that you mean nothing to them;
instead, forgetting everything,
dwell in recollection with your Spouse.

93. *Ame mucho los trabajos, y téngalos en poco por caer en gracia al Esposo, que por ella no dudó morir.*

Have a great love for trials,
and consider them of little importance
since they are pleasing to your Spouse,
who for you did not hesitate to die.

94. *Tenga fortaleza en el corazón contra todas las cosas que le movieren*[29] *a lo que no es Dios, y sea amiga de la pasión de Cristo.*

Be strong in your heart against everything
that could attract you to what is not God,
and befriend the passion of Christ.

95. *Traiga interior desasimiento a todas las cosas, y no ponga el gusto en alguna temporalidad, y recogerá su alma a los bienes que no sabe.*

Approach all things with inner detachment,
and do not seek pleasure in anything temporal,
and your soul will become recollected
in blessings beyond its ken.

96. *El alma que anda en amor ni cansa ni se cansa.*

The soul that walks in love
is neither wearisome nor wearied.

97. *Al pobre que está desnudo le vestirán, y al alma que se desnudare de sus apetitos, quereres y no quereres, la vestirá Dios de su pureza, gusto y voluntad.*

The poor person who is naked will be clothed,
and the soul that casts off
her appetites, preferences and aversions
will be clothed by God
in his purity, pleasure and will.

29 Rodríguez (1993: 104) has 'movieron'.

98. *Hay almas que se revuelcan en el cieno, como los animales que se revuelcan en él,*[30] *y otras que vuelan, como las aves que en el aire se purifican y limpian.*

Some souls roll in the mud,
like the animals that roll in it,
while others take flight
like birds that in the air
make themselves pure and clean.

99. *Una palabra habló el Padre, que fue su Hijo, y ésta habla siempre en eterno silencio, y en silencio ha de ser oída del alma.*

The Father uttered one word,
namely His Son,
and this He utters continually
in everlasting silence,
and in silence the soul must hear it.

100. *Los trabajos los hemos de medir a nosotros, y no nosotros a los trabajos.*

We must make ourselves the measure of our trials,
not our trials the measure of ourselves.

101. *El que no busca la cruz de Cristo no busca la gloria de Cristo.*

A person who does not seek the cross of Christ
is not seeking Christ's glory.

30 2 Peter 2.22: 'The dog is returned to his vomit: and the sow that was washed to her wallowing in the mire'.

102. *Para enamorarse Dios del alma, no pone los ojos en su grandeza, mas en la grandeza de su humildad.*

When God falls in love with a soul,
he does not look at her greatness,
but on the greatness of her humility.

103. *El que tuviere vergüenza de confesarme delante de los hombres, también la tendré yo de confesarle delante de mi Padre, dice el Señor.*[31]

'A person who is ashamed
to acknowledge me before others
I will be ashamed in turn
to acknowledge before my Father',
says the Lord.

104. *El cabello que se peina a menudo estará esclarecido y no tendrá dificultad en peinarse cuantas veces quisiere, y el alma que a menudo examinare sus pensamientos, palabras y obras, que son sus cabellos, obrando por amor de Dios todas las cosas, tendrá muy claro su cabello; y mirarle ha el Esposo su cuello, y quedará preso en él y llagado en uno de sus ojos,*[32] *que es la pureza de intención con que obra todas las cosas. El cabello se comienza a peinar de lo alto de la cabeza, si queremos esté esclarecido; todas nuestras obras se han de comenzar desde lo más alto del amor de Dios, si quieres que sean puras y claras.*

31 Matthew 10.33.

32 Song of Songs 4.9: 'Thou hast wounded my heart, my sister, my spouse, thou hast wounded my heart with one of thy eyes, and with one hair of thy neck'.

Hair that is combed often will shine,
and will be easy to comb
whenever one wishes,
and a soul who examines often
her thoughts, words and deeds
(which are her hair),
and who does all things with love for God,
will have hair that shines brightly;
and her Spouse, gazing on her neck.
will be imprisoned within it
and wounded by one of her eyes,
namely the purity of intention
with which she does everything.
Hair is combed downwards from the top of the head
if we wish it to shine,
and all our deeds should begin
from the high point of our love of God,
if you wish them to be pure and clear.

105. *El cielo es firme y no está sujeto a generación, y las almas que son de naturaleza celestial son firmes, no están sujetas a engendrar apetitos ni otra cualquier cosa, porque se parecen a Dios en su manera, que no se mueven*[33] *para siempre.*

The heavens are stable,
and set free from the need to engender,
and souls whose nature is heavenly
are stable and set free
from giving birth to desires or anything else,
for they are, in their own way, like God,
and are unchanging forever.

33 Rodríguez (1993: 105) has 'mueve'.

106. *No comer en pastos vedados, que son los de esta vida presente, porque bienaventurados son los que han hambre y sed de justicia, porque ellos serán hartos.*[34] *Lo que pretende Dios es hacernos dioses por participación,*[35] *siéndolo él por naturaleza, como el fuego convierte todas las cosas en fuego.*

Do not eat in forbidden pastures,
namely those of the present life,
because blessed are those
who hunger and thirst for justice,
since they will be satisfied.
It is God's intention
to make us divine by participation,
as he is by nature,
like fire that changes all things into fire.

107. *Toda la bondad que tenemos es prestada, y Dios la tiene por propia obra. Dios y su obra es Dios.*[36]

All the goodness we possess is borrowed,
and God considers it his own work.
God and his work is God.

108. *La sabiduría entra por el amor, silencio y mortificación. Grande sabiduría es saber callar, y no mirar dichos ni hechos ni vidas ajenas.*

Wisdom enters through love,
silence and mortification.
There is great wisdom in knowing

---

34 Matthew 5.6.

35 2 Peter 1.4: 'he hath given us most great and precious promises, that by these you may be made partakers of the divine nature'.

36 On 'Dios y su obra es Dios', see Rodriguez (1993: 105). The meaning seems to be, 'God and his work are one'.

when not to speak,
and in not attending
to the words, deeds and lives
of other people.

109. *Todo para mí y nada para ti.*

Everything for me and nothing for you.

110. *Todo para ti y nada para mí.*

Everything for you and nothing for me.

111. *Déjate enseñar, déjate mandar, déjate sujetar y despreciar, y serás perfecta.*

Let yourself be taught,
let yourself be ordered,
let yourself submit and be scorned,
and then you will be perfect.

112. *Cinco daños causa cualquier apetito en el alma: el primero, que la inquieta; el segundo, que la enturbia; el tercero, que la ensucia; el cuarto, que la enflaquece; el quinto, que la oscurece.*

Any appetite in the soul
harms her in five ways.
First, it makes her anxious;
second, it disturbs her;
third, it soils her;
fourth, it weakens her;
fifth, it deprives her of light.

113. *La perfección no está en las virtudes que el alma conoce de sí, mas consiste en las que nuestro Señor ve en el alma, la cual es carta*[37] *cerrada; y así no tiene de qué presumir, mas estar el pecho por tierra acerca de sí.*

Perfection does not lie in the virtues
that the soul knows herself to possess,
but in those our Lord sees in the soul.
She is a letter that has been sealed,
and so has no reason to boast;
she should instead lie prostrate on the ground
in matters concerning herself.

114. *El amor no consiste en sentir grandes cosas, sino en tener grande desnudez y padecer por el Amado.*

Love does not consist in great feelings,
but in being quite naked
and suffering for the Beloved.

115. *Todo el mundo no es digno de un pensamiento del hombre, porque a solo Dios se debe; y así, cualquier pensamiento que no se tenga en Dios se le hurtamos.*

The entire world is unworthy
of a single human thought,
because it is owed to God alone;
hence any thought
not entertained in God
is stolen by us from Him.

---

37 Rodríguez (1993:105) has 'carga', an alternative manuscript reading (*carga cerrada*: a purchase or acquisition whose contents are unknown). Both 'carta' and 'carga' are possible, but 'carta' is more likely in view of St Paul's words in 2 Corinthians 3.3: 'you are the epistle of Christ, ministered by us, and written not with ink, but with the Spirit of the living God; not in tables of stone, but in the fleshly tables of the heart'.

116. *Las potencias y sentidos no se han de emplear todas en las cosas, sino lo que no se puede excusar, y lo demás dejarlo desocupado para Dios.*

Our faculties and senses
should not be busied entirely with things,
but only insofar as is necessary;
otherwise they should be left
unoccupied for God.

117. *No mirar imperfecciones ajenas, guardar silencio y continuo trato con Dios desarraigarán grandes imperfecciones del alma, y la harán señora de grandes virtudes.*

Ignoring the imperfections of others,
keeping silent,
and relating continuously to God
will uproot great imperfections in the soul,
and make her mistress of great virtues.

118. *Las señales del recogimiento interior son tres: la primera, si el alma no gusta de las cosas transitorias; la segunda, si gusta de la soledad y silencio y acudir a todo lo que es más perfección; la tercera, si las cosas que solían ayudarle le estorban, como es*[38] *las consideraciones y meditaciones y actos, no llevando el alma otro arrimo a la oración sino la fe y la esperanza y la caridad.*

There are three signs of interior recollection:
first, if the soul has no taste
for things that are passing;
second, if she relishes solitude and silence,
and is attracted to everything

38 Rodríguez (1993:106) has 'son'.

that involves greater perfection;
third, if she is impeded
by things that once helped her,
such as considerations, meditations and acts,
and has no support in her prayer
other than faith, hope and charity.

119. *Si un alma tiene más paciencia para sufrir y más tolerancia para carecer de gustos, es señal que tiene más aprovechamiento en la virtud.*

If a soul is more patient in suffering
and tolerates more easily of a lack of pleasure
it is a sign that she is advancing further in virtue.

120. *Las condiciones del pájaro solitario son cinco. La primera, que se va a lo más alto; la segunda, que no sufre compañía, aunque sea de su naturaleza; la tercera, que pone el pico al aire; la cuarta, que no tiene determinado color; la quinta, que canta suavemente. Las cuales ha de tener el alma contemplativa: que se ha de subir sobre las cosas transitorias, no haciendo más caso de ellas que si no fuesen; y ha de ser tan amiga de la soledad y silencio, que no sufra compañía de otra criatura; ha de poner el pico al aire del Espíritu Santo, correspondiendo a sus inspiraciones, para que, haciéndolo así, se haga más digna de su compañía; no ha de tener determinado color, no teniendo determinación en ninguna cosa, sino en lo que es voluntad de Dios; ha de cantar suavemente en la contemplación y amor de su Esposo.*

A solitary bird has five characteristics.
First, it travels to the highest part;
second, it cannot bear company, even of its own kind;
third, it lifts its beak into the breeze;

fourth, it has no fixed colour;
fifth, it sings delightfully.
These should be characteristics of a contemplative soul:
she should rise above passing things,
paying them no more attention than if they did not exist,
and be so fond of solitude and silence
that the company of other creatures is unbearable;
she should lift her beak into the breeze of the Holy Spirit,
responding to his inspirations,
in order to become in that way
more worthy of his company;
she should have no fixed colour,
lacking a fixed purpose in anything
except insofar as it is God's will;
and she should sing delightfully,
in contemplation and love of her Spouse.

121. *Los hábitos de voluntarias imperfecciones que nunca acaban de vencerse, no solamente impiden a la divina unión, pero para llegar a la perfección, como son: costumbre de hablar mucho, algún asimientillo sin vencer, como a persona, vestido, celda, libro, tal manera de comida y otras conversaciones y gustillos en querer gustar de las cosas, saber y oír, y otras semejantes.*

Habitual and freely chosen imperfections
that are never overcome
are an obstacle not only to divine union
but to attaining perfection,
such as a habit of talking much,
or some small, unconquered attachment,
for instance to a particular person,
item of clothing, cell or book,

to a specific type of meal,
or to certain conversations;
little preferences in one's desire
to enjoy, know, hear things;
and other imperfections of a like kind.

122. *Si gloriarte quieres y no quieres parecer necio y loco, aparta de ti las cosas que no son tuyas, y de lo que queda habrás gloria. Mas, por cierto, si todas las cosas que no son tuyas apartas, en nada serás tornado, pues de nada te debes gloriar si no quieres caer en vanidad. Mas descendamos ahora especialmente a los dones de aquellas gracias que hacen a los hombres graciosos y agradables delante de los ojos de Dios: cierto es que de aquellos dones no te debes gloriar, que aun no sabes si los tienes.*

If you want to boast,
without seeming simple-minded and foolish,
put aside the things that are not yours,
and in what remains
you will have something to boast about.
Be sure, though, that if you put aside
all the things that are not yours,
you will turn into nothing,
because you should boast of nothing
if you wish to avoid vainglory.
Let's focus now in particular on those gifts of grace
that make people attractive and agreeable in God's eyes:
of those gifts, certainly, you must not boast,
since you don't even know if you possess them.

123. *¡Oh, cuán dulce será a mi la presencia tuya, que eres sumo bien! Allegarme he yo con silencio a ti y descubrirte he los pies porque tengas por bien de me juntar contigo en matrimonio a mí, y no holgaré hasta que me goce en tus brazos.*[39] *Y ahora te ruego, Señor, que no me dejes en ningún momento en mi recogimiento, porque soy desperdiciadora de mi alma.*

Oh, how I shall enjoy your presence,
you who are my greatest good!
I will approach you in silence
and uncover your feet
so that you may be pleased
to unite me with you in marriage,
and I will not rest
until I rejoice in your arms.
And now, Lord, I beg you:
do not for a single moment
abandon me in my recollection,
for I am wasteful of my soul.

124. *Desasida de lo exterior, desaposesionada de lo interior, desapropiada de las cosas de Dios, ni lo próspero la detiene ni lo adverso la impide.*

Detached from things exterior,
dispossessed of things interior,
divested of the things of God,
you are not held back by good fortune,
nor impeded by adversity.

---

39 See Ruth 3.4–9.

125. *El alma que está unida con Dios, el demonio la teme como al mismo Dios.*

A soul united with God
is feared by the devil
as much as God Himself.

126. *El más puro padecer trae y acarrea más puro entender.*

The purest suffering
brings with it and produces
purer understanding.

127. *El alma que quiere que Dios se le entregue todo, se ha de entregar toda, sin dejar nada para sí.*

A soul that wants God to give her everything
has to give herself entirely,
holding back nothing for herself.

128. *El alma que está en unión de amor, hasta los primeros movimientos no tiene.*

A soul in the union of love
lacks even the first movements of sin.

129. *Los amigos viejos de Dios por maravilla faltan a Dios, porque están ya sobre todo lo que les puede hacer falta.*[40]

Old friends of God
hardly ever fail
to do what God requires,
because they have risen above
all they could require themselves.

40 *falta* is the reading in Pacho (1997: 113). Rodríguez (1993: 129) and Ruano (1994: 168) have *faltar*.

130. *Amado mío, todo lo áspero y trabajoso quiero para mí, y todo lo suave y sabroso quiero para ti.*

Everything harsh and laborious
I desire for me, my love,
and everything easy and delightful
I desire for you.

131. *La mayor necesidad que tenemos para aprovechar es de callar a este gran Dios con el apetito y con la lengua, cuyo lenguaje que él más oye, sólo es el callado amor.*

What we most need
if we are to make progress
is to be silent before this great God
in our desires and in our tongue:
the language that he hears most clearly
is none other than silent love.

132. *Desancillar*[41] *para buscar a Dios. La luz que aprovecha en lo exterior para no caer es al revés en las cosas de Dios, de manera que es mejor no ver, y tiene el alma más seguridad.*

To seek God, do without light.
The benefit of the light outside
that stops us falling
is reversed in the things of God,
and so not seeing is better,
and makes the soul more secure.

41 The meaning of *desancillar* is uncertain. It may be a copyist's error (Ruano 1994: 168; Pacho 1997: 113). The alternatives that have been suggested include *desencandilar* (to remove or dim a bright light), a reading that accords with the images that follow in the saying (Rodríguez 1993: 108).

133. *Más se granjea en los bienes de Dios en una hora que en los nuestros toda la vida.*

More things that belong to God
are acquired in a single hour
than we acquire of our own
in a whole lifetime.

134. *Ama el no ser conocida de ti ni de los otros. Nunca mirar los bienes ni los males ajenos.*

Love being unknown
to yourself and to others.
Never dwell on the affairs,
good and bad,
of other people.

135. *Andar a solas con Dios; obrar en el medio; esconder los bienes de Dios.*

Walk alone with God;
in your actions avoid extremes;
conceal the good things God has given you.

136. *Andar a perder y que todos nos ganen es de ánimos valerosos, de pechos generosos; de corazones dadivosos es condición dar antes que recibir, hasta que vienen a darse a sí mismos, porque tienen por gran carga poseerse, que más gustan de ser poseídos y ajenos de sí, pues somos más propios de aquel infinito Bien que nuestros.*

People who are valiant and noble in spirit
are prepared to lose
and to let others win;

and those with generous hearts
are more inclined to give
than to receive,
and end up giving themselves,
considering it a great burden
to possess themselves:
they would rather be possessed,
and estranged from themselves,
for we belong more truly
to that infinite Good
than to ourselves.

137. *Grande mal es tener más ojo a los bienes de Dios que al mismo Dios. Oración y desapropio.*

It is a great evil
to care more for God's gifts
than for God himself.
Prayer and surrender of one's possessions.

138. *Mire aquel infinito saber y aquel secreto escondido. ¡Qué paz, qué amor, qué silencio está en aquel pecho divino, qué ciencia tan levantada es la que Dios allí enseña!, que es lo que llamamos actos anagógicos, que tanto encienden el corazón.*

Consider that infinite wisdom
and that hidden mystery:
what peace, what love, what silence
reside in that divine breast,
and how exalted is the knowledge
God teaches there!
Our term for it is 'anagogical acts'
that so set the heart ablaze.

139. *Mucho se desmejora y menoscaba el secreto de la conciencia todas las veces que alguno manifiesta a los hombres el fruto de ella, porque entonces recibe por galardón el fruto de la fama transitoria.*

The secret of a person's conscience
is greatly impaired and diminished
whenever they reveal its fruit to others,
for then they receive as their reward
the fruit of a fame that is transitory.

140. *Hable poco, y en cosas que no es preguntado no se meta.*

Say little,
and in matters you are not asked about
do not get involved.

141. *Siempre procure traer a Dios presente y conservar en sí la pureza que Dios le enseña.*

Strive to be aware at all times
that God is present,
and to preserve within yourself
the purity that God shows you.

142. *No se disculpe ni rehúse ser corregido de todos; oiga con rostro sereno toda reprensión; piense que se lo dice Dios.*

Do not make excuses
or refuse to listen
when everyone corrects you;
with a serene countenance
give a hearing
to every reproach;

reflect that it is God
who is speaking to you.

143. *Viva como si no hubiese en este mundo más que Dios y ella, para que no pueda su corazón ser detenido por cosa humana.*

Live as if in this world
there were only God and yourself,
and thus ensure that your heart
cannot be held back
by anything human.

144. *Tenga por misericordia de Dios que alguna vez le digan alguna buena palabra, pues no merece ninguna.*

Look on it as a mercy of God
if they sometimes have a good word for you,
for you don't deserve any.

145. *Nunca deje derramar su corazón, aunque sea por un credo.*

Do not let your heart be scattered,
even briefly.

146. *Nunca oiga flaquezas ajenas, y si alguna se quejare a ella de otra, podrále decir con humildad no le diga nada.*

Never listen to accounts
of the defects of others,
and if a sister complains to you
about the faults of another,
you can ask her with humility
to tell you nothing.

147. *No se queje de nadie; no pregunte cosa alguna; y si le fuere necesario preguntar, sea con pocas palabras.*

Complain about no one;
ask no questions;
and if you do have to ask,
use few words.

148. *No rehúse el trabajo, aunque le parezca no lo podrá hacer. Hallen todos en ella piedad.*

Refuse no task,
even if it seems beyond you.
Let everyone find in you
a tender heart.

149. *No contradiga. En ninguna manera hable palabras que no vayan limpias.*

Do not contradict others.
Never utter words
that are not clean.

150. *Lo que hablare sea de manera que no sea nadie ofendido, y que sea en cosas que no le pueda pesar que lo sepan todos.*

Let what you say be said
in a way that offends no one,
and be about things
you don't mind everyone knowing.

151. *No niegue cosa que tenga, aunque la haya menester.*

Do not deny another person
anything you possess,
even if it is something you need.

152. *Calle lo que Dios le diere, y acuérdese de aquel dicho de la esposa: Mi secreto para mí.*[42]

Do not speak about what God gives you,
and remember that saying of the bride:
My secret to myself.

153. *Procure conservar el corazón en paz; no le desasosiegue ningún suceso de este mundo; mire que todo se ha de acabar.*

Try to keep your heart at peace;
do not be disturbed
by any event in this world;
reflect that all things
will come to an end.

154. *No pare mucho ni poco en quién es contra ella o con ella, y siempre procure agradar a su Dios. Pídale se haga en ella su voluntad. Amele mucho, que se lo debe.*

Do not dwell, much or little,
on who is with you or against you,
and always strive to please your God.
Pray that his will may be done in you.
Love him greatly, for you owe him that.

155. *Doce estrellas para llegar a la suma perfección: amor de Dios, amor del prójimo, obediencia, castidad, pobreza, asistir al coro, penitencia, humildad, mortificación, oración, silencio, paz.*

Here are twelve stars to guide you
on the way to the greatest perfection:
love of God, love of your neighbour,

42 Isaiah 24.16.

obedience, chastity, poverty,
fidelity to the hours of choir,
penance, humility, mortification,
prayer, silence, peace.

156. *Nunca tomes por ejemplo al hombre en lo que hubieres de hacer, por santo que sea, porque te pondrá el demonio delante sus imperfecciones, sino imita a Cristo, que es sumamente perfecto y sumamente santo, y nunca errarás.*

When tackling the things you have to do,
never take as your model
a human being, however holy,
because the devil will place before you
their imperfections.
Instead imitate Christ,
who is entirely perfect and entirely holy,
and you will never go astray.

157. *Buscad leyendo y hallaréis meditando; llamad orando y abriros han contemplando.*[43]

Seek in reading,
and you will find in meditation;
knock in prayer,
and it will open for you
in contemplation.

43 This saying is a translation of a sentence in the *Scala paradisi* of a twelfth-century writer, the Carthusian Guigo II: 'Quaerite legendo, et invenietis meditando; pulsate orando, et aperietur vobis contemplando' (Patrologia Latina 40:998; 184:476).

Sayings recalled by Magdalena del Espíritu Santo*

* Magdalena del Espíritu Santo was a nun in the Carmelite community in Beas. She recorded these sayings in a manuscript now in the Biblioteca Nacional in Madrid. See Pacho (1997: 108).

158. *El que con puro amor obra por Dios, no solamente no se le da de que lo sepan los hombres, pero ni lo hace porque lo sepa el mismo Dios; el cual aunque nunca lo hubiese de saber, no cesaría de hacer los mismos servicios, y con la misma alegría y amor.*[44]

Someone who with pure love performs a good act for God,
not only cares nothing about others seeing it,
but does not do it for God himself to know;
even if He were never to know it, such a person
would not cease to serve Him in the same ways,
and with the same happiness and love.

159. *Otro para vencer los apetitos: traer un ordinario apetito de imitar a Jesucristo en todas sus obras, conformándose con su vida, la cual debe considerar para saberla imitar y haberse en todas las cosas como él se hubiera.*

A further saying about mastering appetites:
make your usual appetite the desire
to imitate Jesus Christ in every action
in conformity with his life,
on which you should reflect
so that you can imitate it
and behave in all things as he would.

160. *Para poder hacer esto, es necesario que*[45] *cualquiera*[46] *apetito o gusto, si no fuere puramente por honra y gloria de Dios, renunciarlo y quedarse en vacío por amor de él que en esta vida no tuvo ni quiso más de hacer la voluntad de su Padre, la cual llamaba su comida y manjar.*[47]

44 Another version of saying number 20.

45 Ruano (1994: 170) reads, 'que es necesario'.

46 Rodríguez (1993: 108) and Ruano (1994: 170) read, 'cualquier'.

47 John 4.34: 'Jesus saith to them: My meat is to do the will of him that sent me'.

To be able to do this, you must renounce
every appetite and preference
not directed to God's honour and glory,
and remain in emptiness for love of him
who in this life had and desired nothing
except to obey his Father's will,
which he called his food and choice fare.

161. *Para mortificar las cuatro pasiones naturales, que son gozo, tristeza, temor y esperanza, aprovecha lo siguiente: procurar siempre inclinarse no a lo más fácil, sino a lo más dificultoso, no a lo más sabroso, sino a lo más desabrido, no a lo más gustoso, sino a lo que no da gusto; no inclinarse a lo que es descanso, sino a lo más trabajoso, no a lo que es consuelo, sino a lo que no es consuelo, no a lo más, sino a lo menos, no a lo más alto y precioso, sino a lo más bajo y despreciado, no a lo que es querer algo, sino a lo que no es querer nada; no andar buscando lo mejor de las cosas, sino lo peor, y traer desnudez y vacío y pobreza por Jesucristo de cuanto hay en el mundo.*

To mortify the four natural passions
(namely joy, sorrow, fear and hope),
the following helps:
try to prefer always
not the easiest,
but the most difficult,
not the most agreeable,
but the most unpleasant,
not the most pleasurable,
but the absence of pleasure;
try to prefer not what gives rest,
but what is most demanding;

not what consoles,
but what does not;
not what is greater,
but what is less;
not what is highest and most precious,
but what is lowest and most despised;
not the desire for something,
but the desire for nothing;
try to seek continually
not the best of things, but the worst,
and to practise nakedness and emptiness and poverty
for the sake of Jesus Christ
in all things to do with the world.

162. *Para la concupiscencia, procurar obrar en desnudez y desear que los otros lo hagan; procurar hablar en desprecio y desear que todos lo hagan; procurar pensar bajamente de sí y desear que los otros lo hagan.*

To deal with concupiscence,
try to act without disguise,
desiring that others do likewise;
try to speak of yourself with disdain,
desiring that all do likewise;
try to think of yourself in lowly terms,
desiring that others do likewise.

163. *Tenga fortaleza en el corazón contra todas las cosas que le movieren a lo que no es Dios, y sea amiga de las pasiones por Cristo.*[48]

48 Another version of saying number 94.

Be strong in your heart against everything
that could attract you to what is not God,
and befriend sufferings for Christ.

164. *Prontitud en la obediencia, gozo en el padecer, mortificar la vista, no querer saber nada, silencio y esperanza.*

Promptness in obedience,
joy in suffering,
mortification in looking,
desire to know nothing,
silence and hope.

165. *Refrene mucho la lengua y el pensamiento y traiga de ordinario el afecto en Dios, y calentársele ha el espíritu divino mucho. Léale muchas veces.*[49]

Keep a tight rein on your tongue and your thoughts,
and habitually place your affection in God,
and the divine spirit will set you fiercely on fire.
Read this often.

49 Another version of saying number 79.

Sayings recalled by María de Jesús*

* María de Jesús (de Solís y Mendoza) was prioress in the Carmelite community of Seville. She recorded these sayings in a manuscript now in the Biblioteca Nacional in Madrid. See Pacho (1997: 40).

166. *Levantarse sobre sí, no hacer asiento en cosa en nada.*

Rise above yourself;
seek rest in nothing at all.

167. *Estar vuelta contra sí, airada y jamás parada.*

Be a foe to yourself,
irascible and never pausing.

168. *Huir con el pensamiento de cabe ellas, cerrando la puerta a todas.*

Flee from their company in your thoughts,
closing the door on them all.

169. *Limpio de todas aficiones, pensamientos e imágenes, el dulce canto suspires con compunción y lágrimas.*

Cleansed of all attachments, thoughts and images,
release your sweet song
with compunction and tears.

Further Sayings*

* These sayings are recorded in a manuscript previously conserved in Antequera and now in the Biblioteca Nacional in Madrid. See Pacho (1997: 40–41).

170. *Cuanto más te apartas de las cosas terrenas, tanto más te acercas a las celestiales y más hallas en Dios.*

The more you draw apart from earthly things,
the more you draw near to heavenly things,
and the more you discover in God.

171. *Quien supiere morir a todo, tendrá vida en todo.*

A person who can die to all things,
will have life in all things.

172. *Apártate del mal, obra bien y busca la paz.*[50]

Shun what is evil,
do good
and seek peace.

173. *Quien se queja o murmura ni es perfecto ni aun buen cristiano.*

Someone who complains or grumbles
is neither perfect
nor even a good Christian.

174. *Humilde es el que se esconde en su propia nada y se sabe dejar a Dios.*

That person is humble
who hides within their nothingness,
and knows how to surrender
into God's hands.

50 Psalm 33.15: 'Turn away from evil and do good: seek after peace and pursue it'.

175. *Manso es el que sabe sufrir al prójimo y sufrirse a sí mismo.*

That person is meek
who can bear with their neighbour
and with themselves.

176. *Si quieres ser perfecto, vende tu voluntad y dala a los pobres de espíritu, y ven a Cristo por la mansedumbre y humildad y síguelo hasta el Calvario y sepulcro.*[51]

If you wish to be perfect,
sell your own will
and give it to the poor in spirit,
and come to Christ
through meekness and humility,
and follow him to Calvary and the grave.

177. *Quien de sí propio se fía, peor es que el demonio.*

A person whose trust
is in themselves
is worse than the devil.

178. *Quien a su prójimo no ama, a Dios aborrece.*

A person who does not love their neighbour
finds God abhorrent.

179. *Quien obra con tibieza, cerca está de la caída.*

A person whose good actions
are half-hearted
is close to a fall.

51 Matthew 19.21: 'Jesus saith to him: If thou wilt be perfect, go sell what thou hast, and give to the poor, and thou shalt have treasure in heaven: and come follow me'.

180. *Quien huye de la oración, huye de todo lo bueno.*

A person who flees from prayer
is fleeing from all that is good.

181. *Mejor es vencerse en la lengua que ayunar a pan y agua.*

Mastering your tongue is better
than fasting on bread and water.

182. *Mejor es sufrir por Dios que hacer milagros.*

Suffering for God is better
than working miracles.

183. *¡Oh, qué bienes serán aquellos que gozaremos con la vista de la Santísima Trinidad!*

O how great are the delights we shall taste
on beholding the Blessed Trinity!

184. *No tengas sospecha contra tu hermano, que perderás la pureza de corazón.*

Do not be suspicious of your brother,
or you will lose purity of heart.

185. *De trabajos, cuanto más, mejor.*

When it comes to trials,
the more the better.

186. *¿Qué sabe quien no puede padecer por Cristo?*

What does a person know
who cannot suffer for Christ?

Note on Sources

My translation is based on three Spanish editions of the Sayings of St John:

- **Rodríguez 1993.** *Dichos de luz y amor*, in *San Juan de la Cruz, Obras completas*, edited by José Vicente Rodríguez with notes and introductions by Federico Ruiz, 5th edition (Madrid: Editorial de Espiritualidad), pp. 91–112.
- **Ruano 1994.** *Dichos de luz y amor*, in *San Juan de la Cruz, Obras completas*, edited by Lucinio Ruano de la Iglesia, 14th edition (Madrid: Biblioteca de Autores Cristianos), pp. 153–73.
- **Pacho 1997.** *Avisos espirituales*, in *San Juan de la Cruz, Obras completas*, 5th edition, edited by Eulogio Pacho (Burgos: Monte Carmelo), pp. 89–116.

The three editions differ in their arrangement of the Sayings, and in their numbering; they vary sometimes too in their readings of the text, and often in its punctuation. I have followed the arrangement and sequential numbering in Rodríguez (1993); where there are different readings I have recorded the variants in a note; and in matters of punctuation I have followed my own judgement. The biblical quotations in the footnotes are from the Douay-Rheims translation of the Latin Vulgate Bible, the version St John used.

I have consulted also the versions of the Sayings in the two standard translations of St John's works in English:

- *The Complete Works of Saint John of the Cross, Doctor of the Church*, translated and edited by E. Allison Peers (London: Burns and Oates, 1964).
- *The Collected Works of St. John of the Cross*, translated by Kieran Kavanaugh, O.C.D., and Otilio Rodríguez, O.C.D., 3rd edition (Washington, D.C.: ICS Publications, 2017).

The following is a valuable essay on the origin and content of the Sayings:

- José Vicente Rodríguez, 'Avisos espirituales', in *Diccionario de San Juan de la Cruz*, edited by Eulogio Pacho (Burgos: Monte Carmelo, 2009), pp. 137–145.

On the life, thought and writings of St John, see Colin Thompson, *St John of the Cross. Songs in the Night* (London: SPCK, 2002).

"...a real gem ...from the pen of one of our foremost scholars in Spanish literature who is also a renowned commentator on St John of the Cross."

Vincent O'Hara O.C.D. in: *Spirituality*, Vol. 28, No. 164 (September–October 2022), p. 317.

"We are indebted to Terence O'Reilly for giving us this translation. His combination of meticulous scholarship and great affection for his subject has given us sure access to the wise guidance of a great mystic."

Joseph Kavanagh O.P. in: *Doctrine and Life*, Vol. 73, No. 7 (September 2022), pp. 63–64.

"Professor O'Reilly has done us a great service by preparing this new translation."

Neil Xavier O'Donoghue in: *The Furrow*, Vol. 73, No. 6 (June 2022), pp. 374–375.

"O'Reilly provides a text that is readable, understandable, accessible."

Sarah Newton in: *Mount Carmel*, Vol. 70, No. 2 (Spring 2022), pp. 79–84.

"This is physically a lovely little book – simple and beautifully laid out so that it is a pleasure to use."

Jill Robson in: *The Traherne Association Newsletter*, No. 82 (Spring 2022).